R A G E

A N D

P E A C E

O F

S O U L Z

V O L U M E   I

THE
RAGE
AND
PEACE
OF
SOULZ
VOLUME I

ROSHON T. JACKSON, SR.

MYND
MATTERS

Mynd Matters Publishing
715 Peachtree Street NE
Suites 100 & 200
Atlanta, GA 30308
http://www.myndmatterspublishing.com

ISBN: 978-1-948145-56-5
e-ISBN: 978-1-948145-57-2

FIRST EDITION

I want to thank God who blessed me with a gift for writing. My wife, Michone, and our children for giving me the inspiration to write. I thank my mother and father who provided a balance of love and discipline and gave me the confidence to believe I could become anything I wanted.

Contents

FLOWERS GIVE THEIR TESTIMONY

Let the flowers give their testimony.

History is told from the outlook of the victorious,
Depicting themselves as liberators and bold,
Plundering everything from the conquered,
their children, religion, and golden temples in sub-
conscious minds.

Let the flowers give their testimony
as when they witnessed strange fruit hanging from trees
and Hiroshima and Nagasaki's fiery breeze.

Unarmed men, women, and children singing
the death blues
and school house "terrorists" becoming part of
everyday news.

Let the flowers give their testimony.
Watching the lives of great men and covering their
caskets after their assassinations.

They know all the boys in blue and green, blood
dripping down a few of their seams.

Their boots lifted—the residue of jungle mud, desert
sand and poppy seed fields too

Their souls eternally carrying the memories of fallen
soldiers and the guilt of living through.

Let the flowers give their testimony.
From the Gate of No Return, ships gliding over blood-
soaked tides
Printing presses pushing out posters with *No Irish or
Italians Need Apply.*

Wolves from Washington licking the crimson path on
the Trail of Tears
There's no depth and length for people's hate,
ignorance, and fear.

Let the flowers give their testimony,
As the towers' foundations were broken free and
the nation united out of tragedy,
Then an insatiable quest for revenge became necessity.

Are we wrapped in justice, seeking peace or endless war,
how long will our souls endure?

REMINISCE

I reminisce on how life used to be
and in every instance,
I celebrate its divine simplicity.
I was impressed by the honeybees
building cities in the trees,
At awe of how vigilant the impalas need to be, leaping to
pick up speed when predators want to feed.

Fellowshipping with my potential
as with an old friend,
We were undeterred by hazards, threats of injuries,
death, failure, or trying again.
My innocence and curiosity made me immune to
stereotypes, limitations and the isms of life,
I just wanted to dance, jump, and sing to the eternal
drum of liberty.

I'm free from the complexities of worry, religion, and
financial woes,
I just enjoy running as the grass tickles my toes.

Because I'm a child on the African plain,
I see Kemet, Nubia, just to name a few,
I see everything I can be
and so can you.

BROKEN HEARTED MOM

When the clutches of life toss unthinkable and unexpected circumstances, plunging you deep into the kingdom of tragedy and despair.

Your world is knocked off its axis while the invisible roots of grief pull you miles below the surface of sanity.

With each breath you exhale every ounce of your strength to stand or crawl, you find yourself unable to navigate this jagged, desolate path with no end.

Despite the assurance of your beloved's salvation, they have transcended into the unseen realm of existence.

No graceful words, divine promises or the timing of your next rendezvous with him provide you with any consolation and your ONLY therapy is shedding oceans of tears to bathe your anguished soul crumbling into pieces.

Every passing moment torrential memories overrun your mind, and changing emotions overwhelm you.

You remember the first time you felt his life-force growing inside you… the first time he mumbled momma, his first tooth and step. You remember stroking his head and back while he lay asleep in his crib and when he came to visit he'd curl up at your feet and you rubbed his head. Most of all you'd remember the last time he said momma.

Now you recollect every sound, smell, touch and facial expression he made is re-welded in your mind,
Now every instance with him, despite its insignificance, becomes precious lifelines to his legacy.

It was your greatest earthly assignment as a Holy Vessel to nurture, love and sustain him until he could do so on his own.

You're a MOTHER, a perfect conduit God uses to usher infants' spirits to their physical destination, until they are disengaged from the natural world.

But, as the seconds, minutes, hours, days, weeks, months and years eventually pass, God has already dispatched angels to reassemble your fractured heart, catch every tear; transforming them into peace lily petals that will shower you and your baby when you reach heaven.

DEDICATION TO THE MAN

This is dedicated to the man whose broad shoulders I sat upon; whose lap was my throne as a little boy.

A man whose hands I thought were enormous and I never imagined eclipsing one day.

A man whose strength and dependability was unparalleled and could never be questioned.

A man who knew my voice and rebelliousness would deepen and decided he had to become a villainous blacksmith placing me into the inferno, hammering immaturity and foolishness out of my spirit.

A man whose demeanor was inflexible to excuses, who didn't tolerate the mumbling or whispering of disrespect.

A man whose words were few but poignant, actions weren't perfect but consistent and prepared me for the sacred rite of passage.

A man who welcomed me into the fold of manhood as a friend, receiving my voice as an equal strengthened our bond while he lived vicariously through my uniform with pride.

A man who refused to help
in order to teach me how to manage all my affairs.

A man who laughed and smiled at my trials of
fatherhood always repeating, "They'll come around."

A man who I thought was an eternal oak tree that would
never whither,
but he always said, "I'll be gone one day."

A man who laid in the hospital bed,
surrendered the "S" on his chest so he could be healed
and I could be at peace.

A man I called *Dad*.

DISTORTED HISTORY

Out of the distorted pages of history
Schizophrenic academics prescribed romanticized
tragedies.

Depicting men like me
with cool crusted lava melanin
To be the eternal enemy of everybody.

Now without me! The father of every genealogy!

But I've been deemed void of any redemptive qualities.

As the world justifies misleading people about me

Diminishing my potential of what I could be
But they've got tunnel vision because they'd rather see
me on Sunday or Saturday as an entertainment piece.

I guess this is the safest place for men like me
Anything else
I'm a potential, no, obvious threat of death or serious
injury to their galactic peace,
regardless of what I chose to Be,
the world has petrified me into the distorted pages of
history.

MY PEOPLE'S SOUL WILL RISE

My people's soul will rise as a blazing Phoenix into our new reality.

Spreading our wings, gliding over the continents like children on wet playgrounds.

Taking flight into the cosmos where our perspectives are all-encompassing.

Honoring ancestral men, women and children whose magnitude of existence and contributions are immeasurable and can't be disputed.

We are eternally indebted to every ancestor who plunged to their death into the abyss rather than live in servitude, perished in the treacherous journey of the middle passage, and those broken by the whip, drudgeries of the field or by ambiguous words on lambskin paper.

Deprived of liberty because of a life in bondage suffocated their happiness, potential and destiny.

There were many that succeeded, accomplished and overcame, despite their circumstances.

They were presumed to be anomalies, but we are the descendants of the original extraordinary people.

Men, women and children who died in every war on U.S. soil and abroad, giving a level of bravery, patriotism, morality and quiet resistance that was stronger than the hate and self-righteousness still living in the heart of this country.

They held tight to the hand of this diseased nation, hoping they could reconcile America's soul.

STAGNANCY

Your potential is a stagnant pond,
the perfect breeding ground for cultivating the disease of
mediocracy while it spreads into your thoughts.

Doubting yourself, while critics convince you to wear
the uniform of your adversary, persuading you to
commit sabotage, treason and genocide against yourself.

But within the hemispheres of your mind
let the genesis of a singular thought become the foothold
you need to change the momentum of what you
perceived as a winless war.

As the whispers of rogue neophyte cells, who carry the
sparks of an uncivil revolution are echoed into the
crevasses of your mind and body.

This liberating malignancy will ascend into an
uncontrolled wildfire, bringing every component of your
being under the submission and authority of your soul.
A soul whose purpose is to operate without restraints,
lead this insurrection in order to build, strengthen and
unify a new Dynasty…while annihilating any fragments
of the old regime.

1,000 LIVES

Perhaps you prefer to sit comfortably on the throne
ruling for a thousand years of mediocrity,
governing policies of indecision,
signing treaties because your fear of battle.

Making your excuses become your royal subjects
who applaud any of your monotonous gestures,
impressing them with shallow undertakings,
assuming that your inconsequential existence will gain
the attention of the universe.

But I'd rather live a short life,
chasing purpose up a mountain,
tenaciously stalking her
like a ravenous lion on the hunt.

Crashing into the boulders of defeat,
tempering the heat of rage,
fighting the blitz of cold regrets,
choking with the high altitude of setbacks, overlooking
and ignoring
the bludgeoning of my hand and feet from climbing.

I've hung from many cliffs of turmoil
until the moment I lifted myself to the top.

Purpose must yield, giving me victory.

Exhaling, I watch the midnight skyline majesty.

The clouds are at rest just below the highest peak. From my perspective I can't see the base of the mountain or the path I endured.

I reminisce on my journey.

I had few companions, traveling mostly in solitude.

The invisible and seemly scars didn't callus my heart, but my decisions set my road miles apart from the masses.

I chose to live as if I was going to die in the next instance.

Fearing nothing, saving nothing and regretting nothing for tomorrow is not promised.

Exhausting my life-force with each step, how I live will be a testimony as the universe will archive my life within the stars.

Bear witness when I surrender my last breath to the rising dawn.

CHOOSE WISELY

A carnally-minded man is unbalanced and contentious
in his fleshy ways, but his charisma is seductive.

Massaging the eardrums of my beautiful broken sisters,
who chase the shadows of their fathers' approval and
promise of love.

At a cost of priceless suffering they endure a multitude
of poverty, pain and momentary pleasures.

Submitting themselves to a man's covering without
honor
pledging default loyal to himself.

He will never grow, stand or show up
he prefers to wear the cloak of boyhood.

EMBRACE

From dusk to dawn rise up and embrace your hills, valleys and terrain

Embrace your kinky, curly, soft, straight and coarse hair

Embrace if you've been scorched, baked or simmered by the sun

Embrace if you're plump, thin, thick, muscular or toned

Embrace whatever continent you've come from

Embrace every sense, emotion, and intuition that makes you self-aware

Embrace your sassy sexiness, untapped powers and infinite cosmic mysteries

Embrace your destiny, authority and purpose

Embrace life, whether it be a sprint or marathon

Embrace every perfect imperfection

Embrace the divinity of a baby's hand wrapped around your thumb

Embrace the anchored Sun, the footprints of the somber moon

Embrace the erosion of tragedy and the waterfall of joy expected to come.

DECISION TODAY

She has to make a decision today,
in the same way she evaluates the regrets of her life every
day.

The three biological fathers are long gone,
their family's hearts are full of foolish pride,
choosing to let her and her children fall by the wayside.

Two sons, seven and six… a daughter three,
and she desperately wants a break from motherhood and
all its responsibilities.

So, so tired of waking up with her soul on empty, bank
account on power to the negative degree.

People in the church told her the Lord will provide, but
that's not helping with her thoughts of suicide.

Her tender heart callused with dreadful experiences,
searching for alcoholic and narcotic deliverance.

Her inescapable past buried deep inside,

Is the reason she falls into the web of no good men,
just as broken as she has been.

Men masking insecurities with punches and smiles,
portraying masculinity as real man style.

The wrong examples for any child to see,
making her children accustomed to constant brutality.

She has to make a decision today,
in the same way she evaluates the regrets of her life every
day.

Will she bring life to death
or death to life?

The decision she has to make is out of fear
because whatever decision she makes will make her shed
so many tears.

Terrified tears of the beatings during pregnancy.

Guilty tears from killing her unborn child's destiny.

Tears from anticipating another mouth to feed,
because in her world hope has no descendancy.

She does things people say they would never do,
getting paid to stroll the street to get her children thru.

Every play she makes she loses in life's game,

It's a miracle she's surviving while living under this mountain of shame.

The eyes of her children have seen life taken for less than a penny

And now gunshots don't even startle them because they've heard so many,

But they've accepted their third-class citizenship in the city of savagery,

As she rubs her stomach contemplating another six months of drudgery.

She has to make a decision today,
in the same way she evaluates the regrets of her life every day.

CHILDREN OF YOUTH

Haiku

Children of my youth
Sacredly placed in my heart
Live forever loved

EXPOSED AND IMMERSED

We have been exposed, immersed into this toxic society
and culture.

Relied on strategically planted thoughts, agendas and
realities rooted within us.

Breathing, absorbing these negative vibrations into our
sub-conscious,
feeding our flesh with unfulfilled desires and unsatisfied
expectations.

Examining this parasitical virus mutating us into an
unrecognizable strain of people.

We have perceived our survival while suffering as a leap
into genome evolution,
but it has only plunged our existence into utter madness.

MY QUEENS

My Queens the myth that the King Warriors of our
tribes have lost their resolve is feeding perpetual lies that
been planted and their roots have grown into towering
forests of trees.

Our ancestors' sovereignty, identity, ingenuity and
royalty were taken with sinister intent.

Our people were abducted, tortured then abandoned
deep underneath the forest floor, 10,000 miles and
counting almost touching earth's core.

They justify covering and concealing the truth with the
dirt of a twisted history that continues to nourish a
murderous romanticized legacy.

In the abysmal bowels of the earth we survived with
memories of the shores of our homeland,

Suffering under the physical and psychological crack of
the whip,

Overseers and governments attempted to beat every
millimeter of melanin from our flesh as if it was the root
of evil and not man's Genesis.

BROKEN VICTORY

They don't know or want to see
the brokenness behind my victory.

I'm more than a man with athletic ability,
so tired of being a retreat from your miserable reality.

Am I the only way you can find peace?

You never want me to react when fans spit, harass and
call me names,

But your excuse for them is that it's all part of the
games.

I can never show anger or be upset or have a bad day,
and if I make a mistake it's on the news the next day.

I'm scrutinized, criticized while my community is
accused of producing these thuggish types behavior and
bad attitudes.

I temper my talent, hard work, dedication,
blended with brashness and my style on the court and
fields of play.

Am I nothing else to you except entertainment on
Saturday and Sunday?

You know I'm different when I have on the uniform,
you might say I'm a black unicorn.

Regardless no one is exempt from the peer pressure,
depression and low self-esteem,

Your love for me have boundaries, and the perforated
lines are easily separated based on my ability to operate
within your confines.

When I enter my domain,
It becomes my temporary sanctuary away from the
troubles, toils and complexities of life,

Away from the shroud of lies, deceptions, envy and
strife.

Away from the self-destructive behavior I see,
on north, south, east and westside streets.

Best believe the problems are definitely the same,
whether people's pockets are fat or struggle in that
welfare game.

Because they don't know or want to see,
the brokenness behind my victory.

DARK CONTINENT MEN

Haiku

Dark continent men
pride, pain and revolution
Unique distinction

GO AWAY LITTLE GIRL

Little girl please go away and grow up,

Your false confidence in your hair, nails and make up,
telegraphing uppercuts, hooks, overhand lefts and rights,
delivering sexual TKO's to men just as shallow as you.

Equating sexual prowess to your deep faith in your
curves and crevasses, ability to seduce and deliver better
than Amazon Prime.

Your good days will pass and that man will be staring at
you in his rear view glass.

Pursuing any male with a ball or mic…
calculating your jump to springboard your mediocrity
into notoriety with treacherous comradery, but its
nothing but pure comedy that you're compromising
everything for financial misery perceived as lifelong
liberty.

DARK LIKE ME

My daughter told me
she's proud to be

Like Lupita and Viola
teardrops of the deepest ebony.

She'll always have love
toward our people's lighter shades

But she embraces being a princess
of the beautiful suit of spades.

Looking in the mirror

She loves and believes in what she sees

A dark continent descendant
beautifully infected
with self-confidence disease.

Beneath her melanin
runs the blood of dynasties

We sat watching our reflections in the bluest sea.

She spoke as an elder,
a matriarch with royal descendence sitting at her feet

My daughter told me,
"Daddy, everyone can't handle being dark like me."

IF THAT WAS ME

What I discovered to be is people love to use the term "If that was me"

Most are conditioned to believe that their opinion dictates my everything.

It's strange they spend fifty percent of their time dedicated to my destiny.

The other fifty percent they complain,

It's a shame, because they just have to switch up their effort game.

But they won't you see,

Because other people's opinions dictate their everything.

Criticizing is their religion and they crucify people with their jealousy.

So, they perpetuate this vicious cycle of saying "If that was me."

KNOWLEDGE ABSORBED

With every bit of knowledge I absorb,

It increases my dialect from a high caliber gun into a thermal nuclear bomb,

Transforming me into a weapon of mass destruction with unlimited range.

Unprepared for America's sanctions and boycotts in 1st amendment disguise.

I reminisce on being back in school,
this seems like homework, pop quizzes, mid-terms and final exams.

But it feels like brothers are always being tested in life's class.

I can accept my failure,

Without the pressure of divine responsibility for every community.

My mind, body and soul on the frontline

Exposing truths,

Despising and deflecting these precision guided lies,

And the only way I'll conquer them is if I step out of line.

I refuse to listen to unrighteous people sending to me die.

Ceremonial flag draped across my casket and I don't know why.

I'm taking divine orders from the Creator's heart to my hand.

And I execute those instructions to the T in public with clandestine efficiency.

I'm a Special Forces warrior in a divine army.

EYES OF MOUNT FUJI

Haiku

Heart, a child's vigor

Dragon's wisdom, tiger's strength

Mount Fuji's three eyes

EVERYTHING & NOTHING

I see everything and nothing

Before surrendering what is important to me,
tearing down the mantle of my heart.

I refuse to pledge allegiance
to all the movements, challenges, trends because
everyone is taking the oath of enlistment.

I'd rather be deaf, only hearing God's voice with my
soul,

Blinded by divine glory,

Instead of living many lifetimes with sight and no
vision.

Be speechless,

But let my love speak for itself.

PEEK-A-BOO

You don't want to be exposed,
hiding behind your social media posts.

Inhaling and sniffing every cloud and line

Using your keyboard courage to get you high.

Searching for that daily fix you have to speculate,
criticize and dismiss any personality

That doesn't fit into the cubicle that you regularly sit.

Making them the focal point of your life, so you become
a Facebook, Twitter and Instagram stalker,
or Blogger.

Wasting a majority of the day's sunshine
and your down time.
testifying about other people's life you define as sublime.

And when you, as a follower, can no longer comprehend
because their proximity used to seem like you had the
whole world in your hand,
and you were emotionally feeling the consistent
connectivity

until you became disappointed and their power slips
away.

and they're the reason why you never seemed to break
through,
or have your dreams come true.

But now you're following this new person in the same
way,
Setting your heart up to be broken time and time again.

CANVAS

I met her as an untouched canvas, a shapeless mold of
precious flesh.

I saw the pedestal, frames;
the master artists commissioned their vision.

Through conversation, communion and fellowship,
her energy, spirit, mind and emotions emerged.

It was not her words,
but her motives, her actions and her heart,
painting and sculpting herself into a masterpiece;

A divine work of art.

GO AWAY LITTLE BOY

Go away little boy,

You're no more a man with your superhero t-shirt than a fictitious hero or their secret identity.

Stuck in boyhood, because of a tragedy or mentality that stifled your maturity,

Now you live on the euphoria of playing video games, watching Sports Center encores and updating your fantasy league.

There's not a flicker of intellect in your mind,

But there's an inferno that craves entertainment that never dies.

You're a dark lighthouse surrounded by rocks guiding the stupid and ignorant to your doorstep.

While you stay high, blissfully flaunting your mediocre accomplishments.

I SPEAK AS A MAN

I speak as a man,

Without the luxury of being a Black man with a ball or mic in my hand

I stand on an unrecognized stage

Where my deeds and fruits will give me one hundred percent of a multiple comma pay

I don't have to sanitize any percent of what I do or what I say

Understanding that my armies and enemies stand behind the gates of my eyes

These inferior thoughts undermine my existence

They must surrender and assimilate or die

Succumbing to a superior mindset to liberate myself

That's the only way to win this war

As one is resolute and the other must compromise.

INSTINCTUAL ANGRY

My angry is instinctual savagery and I embrace it.

I upload it into my matrix,
a simple program erupting into an uncontrolled wildfire

Purging the decayed forest of my soul.

Resurrection from the blaze with the sweet aroma of
rage seeping from every pore

I gain clarity from the destruction,

Planting seeds of hatred and discourse into a fertile
ground

I know its roots will consume me

Knocking my sanity from its axis

The pleasure of being on unbalanced ground is euphoric

In daylight I'm blessed with anxiety

Midnight, insomnia befriends me

I have no refuge, solace or peace

Branded an irrational, unreasonable, uncompromising
fool
waiting for the world to burn

I bring two graham crackers, chocolate and
marshmallows and slowly turn

Don't be confused, anger is only a force of nature I
control...

LOST & FREE

Am I lost and free?

Indeed, to a certain degree.

A first-class citizen of an overpopulated country called
Mediocrity

Am I lost and free?

Indeed, to a certain degree.

Constantly recalculating my perspective in order to see,

The false azimuths of my broken philosophy.

Am I lost and free?

Indeed to a certain degree.

Success made me into a prisoner of society,

Scrutinizing my life, people's concealed judgement,
but actually jealousy, preying upon me.

In death I can't hear their praise, adding me to their
superficial monopoly.

Am I lost and free?

Indeed, to a certain degree.

Deciphering the rage of the reality,

Making peace with the mistakes of my history,

Surrendering my life in the abyss of longevity.

IT DIDN'T SEEM

She didn't look like a damsel in distress wearing that
colorful Chanel dress.

It didn't seem like she was interested in me
a husband and father of three.

I didn't know what could become of her flirtatious
compliments and our work-related lunches on the run.

I was focused on my destiny you see,

But I was unaware of her seductive personality.

And I unintentionally placed myself on the road to
infidelity.

Her first touch was innocent you see,
rubbing my hand with a touch of sensuality,

Saying it was so easy to talk to me and she wished her
man was more like me.

It didn't seem like she was interested in me
a husband and father of three.

I should have addressed it, but I didn't you see

And that's when her first hook was dug inside of me.

I should have dropped dime you see,

But I kept this incident in confidentiality.

Maybe she was spoon feeding my ego
or was it my stupid masculinity that lead me to be
deceived.

Underestimating her game was a mistake you see.

She been dropping subtle tactics meant to infiltrate my
thoughts with consistency.

I thought I could resist,
but smiley face notes on my desk,
wearing paparazzi jewelry to accentuate her breast and
her endless appreciation for listening to her complaints
about her relationship mess.

I was just listening to this woman,

It didn't seem like she was interested in me
a husband and father of three.

But my wife would never believe I wasn't contributing
to this woman seeking me as vaccines prey on disease.

She called me crying and angry you see,

Heartbroken from her man cheating on her for a record
two times three.

She said she just needed to get away and was temporarily
staying in the Hilton Suites room 6902.

It wasn't obvious what she wanted to do,
so, I found a few minutes to comfort her, because that is
what good Christians do.

It didn't seem like she was interested in me
a husband and father of three.

When I realized what she had carefully crafted for me I
was an amateur and she was a pro at seductive games
you see.

In the aftermath I was regretted yet craved this thing
unable to understand how I got here you see

After all,

It didn't seem like she was interested in me
a husband and father of three.

SEASONS & TIMES

I've had few friends, associates and many adversaries during the seasons and times of my life.

The greatest teacher journeying with me is my enemy.

The natural enmity between me and thee,

Is the reason I use to walk the path of destruction,

But now I'm running toward my destiny.

I've had few friends, associates and many adversaries during the seasons and times of my life.

Strife, depression and compliancy were acquaintances that communed and commingled with me.

They gave birth to incidents and tragedies whose complexities were arbitrarily,

Controversially designed to distract and sidetrack me into believing in the greatness of mediocrity.

I've had few friends, associates and many adversaries during the seasons and times of my life.

Persevering in a whirlwind existence,

Bending, but not breaking me spiritually.

The weight of misfortune will always burden me,

But the mantle of friendship essentially uplifts me.

Nothing can prevent the ebb and flow of life,

I appreciate the few men that stuck closer to me than a
brother
giving the reassurance that comforted my soul.

FRACTURED HEART

Life-givers have endured, suppressing their own self-interests, suffering silently, gaining quiet strength.

With wounded souls crying into the everlasting wind, praying it will carry their righteous anger and grievances to the alter of justice to be heard.

Not to gain attention, deliver criticism, produce controversy and definitely not to despise or sensationalize.

Their voices are unified and can't be contained, erupting fiery ash into the white clouds scattering quicker than cosmic rays over each horizon.

Exposing the subtle, ambiguous and unscrupulous behaviors and languages that linger and plague this patriarchal culture, drastically increasing the visibility of well know secrets.

Let thunder and lightning knock the earth from its axis, followed by seasons of uninterrupted rains of truth that will erode the misconception that to protect manhood we must desecrate womanhood.

Convict the hearts of the silent, choke the arrogant with their own words.

And for the heartless, vile perpetrator,

let the soles of his feet become metal stones while he descends sluggishly into a scorching lake of truth.

Filling his lungs with magnesium cinders, flooding his mind with every ounce of anguish he delivered upon his victims a thousand-fold.

Hell's minions await his arrival, opening the gates and welcoming him with torture.

Let him plead for the tears of his victims to cool his thirst and extinguish his blazing flesh.

Reaching his final place of eternal unrest, his spirit becomes a conduit of agony, slowly anchored to the sun's inferno.

A SISTER THAT GLOWS

Brothers, you ever met a sister that glows,
whose character, elegance and energy flows?

A sister that captivates the world wearing the most frugal
or expensive style,
displaying that infinite to everlasting ivory smile?

Unique in every shade
whether baked, simmered, or barely touched by the Sun,
a sister that can maneuver in any arena and still have
fun.

You'll standby watching her swaying
the high and low tides on the outside of her thighs.

There is nothing artificial about her and how she
embraces her womanly intuitions
with grace, style and effortless precision.

When the windows of her soul enchant you
and her perfect lips speak truth, love and peace everyone
and everything under heaven must cease.

Ivy League institutions can't analyze,
synthesize or comprehend her sassy sexy swag,
admiring her surface beauty

as waves on the oceans' dance.

Too afraid to plunge deep into the abyss
to discover where a true priceless treasure exists.

Even her imperfections are beautifully adorned

You can't appreciate a rose without the thorns.

So, brothers if you're fortunate enough
to be in the presence of a sister that glows,
chase her until the north wind no longer blows.

Pursue her beyond the brink of your existence, when
your heart no longer receives the crimson roaring sea.

Exhale your last breath
to fill your lungs with thoughts of her,
your soul will almost depart its temple
and she'll stop running, embracing you
while the eyes of the cosmos shifts it focus.

I have been favored and privileged
to marry a woman that glows
and blessed to raise women that glow.

WHEN SHE THINKS

When she thinks restating and reemphasizing her
strength and independence
while chasing unachievable images of beauty in her sub-
consciousness

When she thinks the hair, nails, makeup, heels and
clothes defines her
instead of enhancing and polishing a rare gem

When she thinks an ignorant and over-the-top attitude
to everything is the first and only option

When she thinks her mind has no value, but her curves
and crevasses are infinite oil wells

When she thinks age is her enemy and not her ally

When she thinks the silver hairs, wrinkles, stretch marks
on her stomach, butt and thighs, the extra weight years
of motherhood and marriage come as a surprise

When she thinks that a man who has no integrity,
character and loyalty to keep martial vows to his wife or
commitments to his children will keep his promises to
her.

When she thinks it's safe to hitchhike to happiness for a
chance to be free, but life will serve her with a dose
reality.

LIONESS QUEEN

I need a lioness to be Queen of my pride,
with jaws that spit roars and snarls that intimidate.

Teeth that rip flesh and break bones,
yet gentle enough to carry cubs, massage words to
intoxicate my heart and soul.

I succumb to her bold eyes piercing the darkness,
keen ears discerning the vibrations on the Sahara and
cosmic plain.

Her powerful silhouette stalks her ambitions endlessly,
prowling through life with divine purpose.

She occupies two dimensions simultaneously.

In the light she is sovereign in the City of Savagery,
rigid, turbulent, merciless.

In the darkness, the brightest star in the night, peaceful,
flexible, ruling with grace and love.

INCOMPREHENSIBLE

I was asked to parallel her essence, beauty and divine
presence.

Her soul, an uninterrupted volcano,
an overflowing life force with the passion and purpose of
womanhood.

She's a sculptured masterpiece,
her smile a priceless work of art against a cosmic canvas
for the sun, moon and stars.

Encompassing the entire spectrum,
she can be the brightest ebony to the darkest mahogany.

Her worth greater than rubies, diamonds and pearls; her
depth a bottomless oil well syphoning kindness,
gentleness and love into others more than herself,

Demonstrating she's the mother of humanity because
Mortal words wouldn't define her spirituality.

PEARL'S DEPTH

Knowledge is reserved for those that desire to nurse from her breast, absorb her energy and listen for her song.

She bears the sweetest fruit and her treasures are priceless.

As infants fear, they search for the divine mother's eyes in new surroundings, recognizing her heartbeat and soothing touch.

Do you believe she can be limited from Genesis to Revelation?

How much does Everlasting to Everlasting encompass and how do you measure it length and depth?

Don't waste your time and words on people whose thoughts aren't deep enough to submerge a pearl.

They desire you to conform to their standard, operate within their limitation, and live for their approval.

They give themselves self-appointed seniority because they've attended places of worship for hundreds of Sundays,

But they are no closer to Heaven than if they built a mansion on Mount Sinai.

WHAT ALLOWED ME TO SURVIVE

What allowed me to survive the genocides of my people?

Flooding my heart with mixed emotions, cursing my thoughts and invading my soul with the unholy guilt of survival.

I was not greater or less than the others who succumbed to life's tragedies.

When hate overshadowed my existence as infinite, unapologetic indifference.

I am never defeated in death; I am the Phoenix.

Where was the infancy of your eternal defiance?

Mine was shackled on the shores of Africa, trodden Trail of Tears, packed railcars headed north, soaked with tears.

In underground jungle tunnels where I defeated two nations with superior technology,

My resolve chose death over surrender. Crawling up on the muddy shadows, grabbing them by the belt buckle.

A stench that your soul will always remember

Center yourself in that reality.

NOT THE AUTHOR OF MY GIFT

I'm not the author of my gift,
but a soul equal to yours.

I've accepted my triumphs, failures, disappointments
and successes because this is the price of transcendence.

Journeying from this realm into another
my mind, body and soul have been interjected with a
subliminal force through divine cross-threading.

When my eyes are opened, I'm asleep,

When my mind is at rest, my subconscious reigns free of
boundaries.

Uplifted from its temple, traveling great distances
without moving, straddling the tight rope of death.

I gain access to cosmic mysteries, absorbing complete
knowledge until...

I'm exiled back into my earthly realm and the memories,
images and knowledge quickly disintegrate from
existence.

THIRST FOR TRUTH

How can you thirst for truth drinking from the well of lies?

Hydrating your self-absorbed soul with conjecture and conspiracies

whose merit's depths are perceived as tidal waves against your shores,

but are truly inconsequential controversies contrived by distractors.

MY THOUGHTS

Your mahogany skin represents the dark recesses of the universe and its mysteries.

Your smile, a thousand supernovas exploding with heavenly glory.

Your eyes, a pair of dazzling comets circling my soul.

Your curves and crevasses are divinely placed constellations measuring perfection.

Your walk; confident, powerful and seductive as a lioness

Your voice, a calming breeze, an explosive gust of wind tempering your faith, that's oceans deep.

Your mind is open like the wingtips of soaring birds.

Your heart, the holy of holies, a buried treasure and I alone know its location.

QUAINT SHALLOWNESS

Is it for my benefit I surrender
my God, my will, lands, possessions, customs, sacred
way of life to a legacy of people infatuated with my
demise or eternal submission?

Drowning me in the quaint shallowness of assimilation
for centuries where I chose second class citizenship
instead of death

Emancipate me in the name of freedom, then send Jim
Crow to oppress me

Appoint cowardice patty rollers to christen me with
insults and stereotypes, provoking me to unleash my
hidden rage

Murdering my brothers and sisters as if they were
buffalo grazing, claiming no meat or hides just their
deaths as a prize.

COLD WHISKEY

Cold whisky escaping my hand
burning the asphalt off my esophagus gland

One by one turning each upside down,
building glass pyramids with no Egyptians around.

Earth's axis spinning, my words jumbled,
vision blurred;
legs were Jell-O but I was fine,

I gotta stay focused on that white, or was it yellow,
striped line.

I swear Lord, I swear I'll never drink again
if you just clear me a path home

Free of roadblocks, check points, traffic and other
drunks like me

Scuba diving inside the abyss of Tennessee's finest
whiskey

I'm a liquor connoisseur, placing one foot after another
to my back door.

Timing, the swaying back and forth trying to go inside

That's when I was rushed from behind.

As quickly as the dawn surrenders to the dusk,
knocked unconscious as if I was steam rolled by a bus.

Awakened by the earth's cold sting,
face down, unable to open my eyes;
it was a darkness that only the condemned had ever
seen.

Stretching my hand out for sanctuary,
it was stopped by a dirt wall

Then the flavor of clay biscuits and root beer treats
overwhelming my tongue,
sending fear from my head to my feet.

Was I robbed,

Beaten?

Because that is the standard nourishment for all of the
dead.

Then, it was her voice,
the voice that tormented me.
I could hear her say

You are a drunk and you're getting everything you deserve anyway.

Please, I'm begging you, please give me another chance,

I just need more time to become a better man.

I'll get another job,

Go to church every day,

I'll even give my blood and plasma for no pay,

I just need more time to become a better man.

I'm begging you, begging you for another chance.

I didn't want to be living and die in a dirty tomb.

Okay, okay all is forgiven

But we're definitely not cool,

And let this be the last time you knock over my flower pots you damn fool.

WHAT'S A BLACK MAN TO DO?

What's a Black man to do when they mention those
select cities that my southern ancestors migrated to?

You know, Chicago, New York, Detroit and LA just to
name a few.

America recognizes them as the drug, poverty and crime
capitals every day, better known as Hood USA.

They've long forgotten about these places, bottled them
up as toxic waste,

Buried the strife, determination, hate and anger far away
from their nightly resting place.

But their intentional deeds sprouted consequential seeds.

And I don't want to succumb to the "I don't give a
damn" disease.

What's a Black man to do, when your only inheritance
is hundreds of years of rage being passed down to you?

Because you feel like you want to cry,
but that weakness will get you set up to be the victim of
a homicide.

Choosing to live and not die is my divine attitude,

On 24 hour watch inside this fortress of solitude.

NEVER KNEW THE STRUGGLE

We knew the agony of struggle, swimming in oceans of mud
nearly succumbing to malignant tides.

Our nostrils were nearly overwhelmed by the stench of hopelessness,

We chose to breath the aroma of opportunity.

When crumbs were the only tangible things to eat,

We endured on the taste of ambition.

During torrential setbacks and disappointments,
we covered ourselves with the umbrellas of brighter days
to come.

Despite our ability to see, shrouded with inadequacies,

Our vision searched for empowerment to lead our way.

When our vocabulary and comprehension was incomplete

We still spoke and stood on what could be.

HARDSHIPS

Son, some of the hardships you'll suffer will seem
unbearable.

Your rite of passage reward for entering manhood is
shedding inadequacies from life,

After the world has expelled you,
reducing you to a feather's floating journey
in the fierce breeze with no end.

Mentally shipwrecked and spiritually dehydrated,

Starving for an ear to listen but your tongue is void and
body is paralyzed.

When you at last think that all is forgotten and all the
tangibles are dissolved,

Let your soul cry out into the heavens

And fall upon the heart of the divine Creator,

Sending transformative thoughts and vibrations to
minister to you

So, you'll be renewed with our love and every word preceding from your mouth.

Believe

Envision

Believe

Speak and Fight your way into victory.

NO MISTAKE IN YOUR CREATION

I made no mistakes in your creation
as I wrapped you in the endless dark cosmos,

No golden ratio equation
is my prerequisite to beauty or excellence.

I created knowledge so you will have keen
understanding and dominion over your physical temple
and nature.

I imparted a portion of my celestial power to you so you
will have intra-standing of your magnificent soul.

I give it to you freely although during life you will try to
distance yourself from my omnipresence.

I designed you with an ability to reverse engineer your
thoughts and actions.

My words designed you in one dimension and
manifested you in another.

COMFORTABLE WITH MY BLACKNESS

Be comfortable with your blackness,
regardless if your birth was intentional,
unexpected or out of tragedy, your destiny resides with
your DNA.

Searching your melanin, you'll discover it to be a fortress
of solitude and solace where you can seize power and
authority in your own existence.

Confidently disembark from this world's programming,
propaganda and discourse meant to distract you into
mental apathy.

MAUSOLEUMS

Reminiscing on my transition from boyhood into manhood I discovered the path I was traveling in life was an elaborate deception.

My indoctrination was an intentional, but delicate programming uploaded brick by brick into my sub-consciousness through my six senses.

Entombing my thoughts, perceptions, passions, reasoning, instincts and discernment within a mausoleum.

Buried alive, six feet deep…terrified.

I pierce the casket lid, welcoming the heavy, moist soil filled with roots and worms.

Struggling to ascend, refusing to look backward because there is no life present below me.

My hand breaching the plot, pulling myself out of obscurity.

I've been resurrected from a lifeless existence.

I arise, lurking amongst the tombstones, observing the earth's restless souls, the mist covering the graveyard.

They drag their un-manifested fortunes like a pendulum within cemetery boundaries.

A SOUL FOR DOWRY

Haiku

Captured by her gaze
My dark queen of the cosmos
Your dowry, my soul

EXILED FROM YOUR SMILE

Lost and forgotten,

Exiled from your smile.

Standing upside down against the Antarctic wind

My rigid soul, searching everlasting to everlasting,

Coming back, looking again and again.

Unmistakably I exist,

Without you, I'm not alive,

Because you gave me life's energy.

Your warm presence was the centerpiece over the mantle of my heart,

Your love for me was a raging inferno that I diminished into a spark.

My infidelity confirmed I didn't know how bright your star burned.

I should have been a martyr for you, a lifetime of
crusades at every turn.

You're not one in a million, billion or trillion,
in hindsight I add endless zeros to your position.

You're one in infinity,

A divine mathematical anomaly,

Now I've created this simple equation.

Suffering through the regrets of my chosen lifestyle,

Lost and forgotten,

Exiled from your smile.

UNMEASURED INFERNO

The unmeasured inferno raging in her heart

Can I consume its fury,
or will it tear us apart?

Will our love become a masterpiece,
or will it become an unfinished work of art?

I listen to the pulsing flame,
laughter, sorrow and pain.

Reminiscing on the years spent
spilling blood, sweat and tears.

Tunneling through the pit of wretchedness with our
hands, hearts, and spirits,

We discovered the journey was only meant to reveal
our true existence.

PAWNS

Are we all pawns while this world plays an eternal game
of chess with the truth?

I don't regret to inform you, I have traded in my
regiments for the most powerful piece on the board, the
Queen.

I won't victim blame, burn and decry why,
why would that guy do that?

Why?

Some don't ask why because they don't assume guilt,
they assume that no one can be that horrible, despicable.

We know about the prowling eyes as she walks by,
unwanted hands rubbing between her thighs,
unwelcomed grabbing of her backside.

After a man ravages a woman's mind, body and soul,

imprinting parasitical spirits draining her of the joys of
life, sadistically gifting her with anguishing memories of
the stench of his breath, demonic gazes in his eyes,
tentacles choking her to incapacitation, then committing
sacrilege inside her temple.

When he finishes feasting and her soul has been reduced to a mustard seed.

For a time, the slightest touch from family, friends or a stranger is the handshake of a leper.

For a time, she will safeguard herself, withdrawing into the purgatory of life

Now like many before her, she has been initiated into the unwanted sorority of defilement, which no one wants to be a member.

This culture devalues, dishonors and decommissions the true purpose of women and girls.

I pray that ignorance or tragedies of this world will not decide your fate or destiny.

SOUTHERN GIRLS

It's something special about them Southern girls

You know them ladies living below the Mason-Dixon line,

Every sister has a generation or two of country in their bloodline.

They so down to earth and always have a smile,

Sitting on their front porch just to talk to you for a while.

Confidence in who they are and what they want to be because God ordained her destiny.

Carefree about the way they add sugar,
baby and honey to the prefix and suffix of what they say,

Analyzing the most complex things into the simplest phrase,

But she gives God all the praise.

Confessing no shame in her southern dialect, draw and twang,

Divine pride in her country name.

Whether she fixin' to cook or bout to go somewhere,

She just rolls up her sleeves and pulls back her hair.

Whipping up gourmet meals with plenty of time to spare.

Even the Ritz-Carlton's hospitality can't compare.

Flexing her skills doing Big Momma's, Momma's and lil' mama's hair.

And when you in trouble,
and on the edge of despair,

She can get a prayer through with the man upstairs.

Fashioned with style, honor and grace,

Loving all people unconditionally regardless of their race.

Diplomatic swag in the way she wears her cool,

But don't be mistaken she can throw them hands and cut a fool.

It's something special about them Southern girls,

God made them perfectly bold,

Imperfect with hearts of gold.

MEMORY FEIGN

I'm a memory feign when it comes to this love thang.
For this love thang I'd be willing to inject, inhale, and
sniff Schedule 1's finest.

For this love thang I march to the cadence of your touch
sending explosive sensations in me all at once.

For this love thang I'd feast on the appetizers of your
kisses, entrees of your heart and soul, desserts of
intermission pursuing record breaking encores.

For this love thang I pursue the aroma of our erotic
brew, infusing my endorphin with sensual rocket fuel,
but there's no hangover after binge drinking with you.

For this love thang, a reward for my persistence
overcoming your flirtation resistance,

this love thang makes your mind indifferent, because
your body's insistent on inviting me into your temple of
pleasure tonight.

INDELIBLE

Was it his indelible, delectable honeysuckle words that
fed your starving soul?

A soul that has been defeated and left desolate by the
scavengers of your past.

His heart dug bottomless spring wells that quenched the
everyday thirst of the Sahara.

His lips, the cool breeze pushing back beads of sweat
from your head.

His touch is the wildfire engulfing your frigid soul.

LOVE'S ANTIQUITY FLICKERING

Suppressed images of our love's antiquity awaken in my sub-conscious mind

Revealing every trace of her existence throughout time

The outward portions of our love that can't be shown

Unforeseen reasons why our love align

With every spark of life we extinguished
there was the frequent burden of discovering and losing each other once again

The adolescence seeds of destiny caught up in the eternal wind

Now our roots have been firmly planted and the countless millennium of pain have ceased.

We now have unspeakable, indescribable life of divine peace.

KINDRED SPIRIT

Haiku

Your kindred spirit
Confounds and compromised me
Whisper my name love

TRANSCENDENCE

My love for you has transcended a multitude of lives, deaths and resurrections.

Its seeds were planted at antiquity, sprouting then spreading its roots until our meeting was destiny and not déjà vu.

The cruelty of pursuing our love endured bondage, distance of war and the trauma of loneliness.

Standing in the valley, we heard the echoes of love's promises ricochet from mountaintop peaks.

But love's everlasting depth and width was patient.

Here on earth together, all our existences spinning in a spiritual tumbler, unleashing repressed memories but never revealing the experience itself.

Today we have deciphered this mystery, we rejoice, as the universe celebrates with us.

Eventually our branch's strength will wither as we are gently pruned from the tree of life.

Lifted by the cosmic wind, carried and planted in another fertile ground to be the first.

Experiencing the birth of the earth, first to reverence a glorious sunrise, smell the first April rain, the first to hear birds singing and waves crashing, the first to admire the northern lights in the midnight sky.

There can be no firsts without you and me because our lives were intertwined into an eternal destiny.

LETTER FROM YOUR CREATOR

Your gifts, purposes and talents have been equally divided.

I did not grant any person a higher platform to display their gifts.

I have no respect of people or gifts.

Never be envious of anyone who has connected with what I have imbedded inside of them.

I created a nature that's driven by instincts and continuous cycles.

They have no choice but to be the best version of whatever I've assigned to them, and they live and die within that sphere of redundancy.

But I fashioned you with free will, you've chosen to live below expectations.

Striving to be fulfilled by insignificance, living but in a dead existence because you're craving to be everything I didn't design you too be.

Struggling with layers of acceptance,

because you want others to accept you,
but you won't accept yourself.

Quit wasting your life masquerading, snipping, cutting,
injecting and enhancing every part of yourself except
your soul.

You can only hide in the shadow of your insecurities in
morning,
but in midday, well into the twilight you'll be
overshadowed by them.

FAR GREATER THAN ME

I declare and decree that the Black Woman is far greater
than me
yes, I said it that she, the Black Women is far greater
than me.

Is it perverted superiority that's invading your mind,
or callous intelligence and inhumane physical prowess,
expecting every woman to be a damsel in distress or
spoiled naïve princess?

I'm resolute in electing to take this stance,
so don't worry

I haven't elevated a second-class citizen flag.

My perspective is liberated and free,
absent of any sincere apologies.

I must address the slight to the enormous injustices that
continue to thrive
and destroy the misogynistic attitudes
that allow predators thrive.

Children are the jewels of every kingdom
but the sacred mines they are birthed from
are valued as hollow caves after excavation

and simple brothel resources
meant to fulfill the pleasures of men.

The elderly are the universe's chroniclers
and Men are its protectors.

All are the beneficiaries of Women.

They are gatekeepers standing guard for our entrance
into this earthly domain.

No one else is suited for this assignment,
only a divine vessel ordained for you and me
with physically, emotional, and heavenly connectivity.

What type of world would despise the Temple
in which every soul must rise?

1,000 SUNRISES AND SUNSETS

For a thousand sunrises and sunsets,
we strayed while we navigated the world,
never sensing, hearing a whisper
or catching a glimpse of each other's presence.

We were content with maintaining the order
and balance of our reality,
determined to live a life of normalcy.

But divine providence ignited a thousand suns shifting
our paradigm in space and time.

When you, the Uncontrolled Blaze,
and I, the Unconquered Soul, intertwined,
it was no coincidence,
but a prophetic consummation between phenomenal
and an anomaly.

At our inception, neither of our wills would yield while
we negotiated matrimony.

Walking and crawling a serrated path together for
years…

A path that finally lead to a mountaintop cliff.

With our hands and feet littered with bruises and
calluses of mistakes.

Without hesitation, leaping toward the heaven together,
breathing new air,
awakening new thoughts, flying over the traveled road
we reminisce over the pain,
but it does not overwhelm our joy.

We've elevated our perspectives,
soaring amongst the doves,
we recognize we're designed for flight,
built to withstand high winds and turbulence.

Our internal pressure is greater
than a supersonic jet puncturing the skies.

Accelerating, climbing higher than ever,
penetrating the atmosphere into the realm of space.

When you, the Uncontrolled Blaze,
and I, the Unconquered Soul,
return home into the cosmos,
we transcend into the speed of sound and light exploring
every new corridor of our existence and the universe.

HIGH GROUND

Haiku

Stand the high ground view,
Watching undressed parts of you
Glisten by the rain

DIME PIECE

Brothers, you're thinking you're going to find that
infamous dime piece.

Because you've been sidestepping rubies who are
priceless and flawed,
but well above satisfactory.

These Dimes got some of these brothers so shook,

Because it's so easy for her to do,

Bouncing and rubbing them 36 double D's while
dancing with you.

You thinking her beauty
and that booty elevates her to a pedestal status quo.

The fellas keep telling you she's a dime piece
and that's the way you should go.

Word on the street is, she's a beast between the sheets.

Greek mythology running deep in her bloodline,

One look, turning your little manhood into stone

But all your ego wants to hear is her scream and moan,

And say, "It's yours baby and yours alone."

That's funny you see, she told the last three suckers, I mean Men, the same thing.

She's a woman of opportunity and looking for you to invest a capital seed

That will produce a return of investment

So let's calculate this thing and see

First you going to be paying her alimony and lawyer fees,

Then twelve-monthly payments times eighteen,

Ooh don't forget about college for four more years.

While you're drunk in regret shedding all those financial tears.

Find a woman that's a friend
with a different set of opinions that don't offend,

But makes you realize and say
"what the hell was I thinking to do and say them things"

A dime piece gives ten and takes ninety away,

So, when you meet her,
she's sending you invitations with those bedroom eyes,

Ready 24/7 to serve the gourmet dish between her
thighs.

If I could surmise
the market place price for sex with her is unaffordable
today,
and the best advice I can give you
is to tell her you about to be on your way.

MOTHERS

Mothers

Beautiful black mothers who raise royalty
and women who stand in gap to be surrogates
to the children in churches, communities, schools and
college campuses

Mothers who speak with uneducated, simple and
sophisticated dialects
whose words and fruits command respect,

Mothers who labored, long suffering in midnight
prayers with tears rolling down their eyes

Mothers whose candles burns at both sides

Women who know they need men to get the nation's
destiny fulfilled

Women that will go out of their way to put a smile on
your face or prepare a home cooked meal

Women who can squeeze another hour into a twenty-
four-hour day
making time to listen to whatever it is you have to say

Mothers that possess a heavenly perspective despite having a child with an attitude that's out of place

Women that never lose faith that God's grace and mercy can deliver that child from a disgrace.

NEGLECT

Haiku

Children of neglect
Desensitized to trauma
Accustomed to pain

AFFAIR WITH HIM

I caught you staring at each other.
What should I do about this affair?

He's fulfilling a void I can't.
He knows the ebb and flow of your soul.
His hands caress your cheeks and stroke your hair.

He memorizes every seam, curve, and dimension of your
ebony face.

He embraces your imperfections even when you don't.

He's intrigued, calling you for a midnight rendezvous,
discovering deeper layers of your beauty and worth.

Your voice and heartbeat have always been his cosmic
anthem.

When the tides of his dreams rise,
you are the moon to balance him.

You're his morning with blue or gray skies,
his night with a backdrop of mythical constellations.

He worships you as a Goddess.
Him…a citizen of a holy temple, a divine heir,
Our son.

PAST MEMORIES

Nothing can separate them from my love.

I loved them before the thoughts of them existed before
it entered my youthful mind,
before God commissioned their spirits and manifested
their births.

I'm resolute and not swayed by their ignorance,
arrogance, or belligerence during adolescence or
adulthood,
And painful as it could be, I can love them from a
distance if need be.

But, eventually, my sight will diminish,
Memories will fade,
And my heart will answer God calling my soul.

I will miss them because we can no longer sit, talk, and
laugh together.

We can't make new memories.

They'll have to reminisce on the days, months, and years
that have passed.

Those past recollections will be the infinite wind,

The eternal crashing tides.

In my life I enjoyed many sunrises and will surrender to a final sunset.

I'll transcend, but my words and love will live within all of you, forever.

IS GOD ELECTRICITY

Is God electricity?

And the only conduit we must use is the church,
customs, traditions, and religiosity?

But how do I get power into this temple filled with
rage, peace, depression, and unmet desires,
Laughter, joy, and low self-esteem?

I could go on for an hour until I name the isms or
condition that have you confined.

Are you afraid to travel to the recesses of your mind?

THE PRIZE

Everybody wants the prize.

Blind to the first-place ribbon in the sky.

Even Christ had second thoughts of His home-going
sunrise.

His tunic stained with blood,
sweat racing from His cheeks to His knees.

He wanted to spill that cup,
But embraced it,
turning up the triple shot of 1800,
tormented pain with no lemon lime chase.

Listening to thirty pieces of silver clanging in the midst,
while the Passover snitch delivered a venomous kiss.

He surrendered,
but He could have summoned His father to assist,
who could have sent natural disasters, legions of arch-
angels and that Ark of the covenant

...shhh....

Instead, remaining silent while His charges were read,

Listened to what His accusers' paid witnesses said.

Jesus said He could knock this temple down and rebuild
it in three days.

You know the story and who they took Him to see,
Claiming Jesus had assumed the title of king.

They said He was perverting the nation and forbidding
people to pay tribute to Rome on any day.

Let me pause for a moment or two,
Back then the Romans were rulers of the Jews,

They saw themselves as benevolent oppressors allowing
them to keep their cultures, customs, and religious
attitudes.

But one condition,
pay taxes worse than receiving private prison phone calls

Deferring ten unsubsidized student loans

Getting a used car with a five hundred thirty-four credit
score.

Okay, let's get back to the story at hand,
Pontius Pilate wasn't a stand-up man,

But he saw straight through the accusation they couldn't prove.

He was curious and asked,
What did this Jesus do?

When they didn't answer, he decided to conduct his own interview.

He determined and found no fault in this Jewish dude.

But the Pharisees and Sanhedrin had the crowd's ear,
they shouted, "Crucify Him! Crucify Him!" with sinister cheer.

So Pilate washed his hands so he could sleep.

Condemned an innocent man and set a murderer free.

The beating that time wouldn't forget,

Thirty something lashes to remove His flesh,

Mocking Him with a crown of thorns, unknowingly signifying, He rules the world.

WATCH AND WONDER

I watch and wonder why the red, green, and orange
leaves tumble free from the trees

Were they held captive by the branches, did they
sacrifice themselves just to be caught up in the wind?

Was each leaf a singular soul?

Or was it a portion of a collective entity of countless
souls?

Is it their true purpose to be on display,

Journeying for thousands of miles or a few feet on the
breath of God into their destiny?

Surrendering nutrients and disengaging their spirits back
into the earth, peaceful as the sunrise and sunset.

Patiently awaiting their reincarnation,
strong, flourishing in the rainy spring,
primed for 1000 Julys
but only lasts 101 days until Fall arrives.

CARIBBEAN NIGHTS

The Caribbean's summer night's heat
drives her into the clear blue sea

Plunging deep only to breach the watery fortress

Bathing her smooth dark skin
glistening from the moonlight and stars
but I am her single audience

I'm mesmerized by the beads of sweat and water
saturating her white linen dress

Confidently relieving her eyeglass figure of this
burdensome attire

Wearing only womanhood
beauty and the simplest jewelry

Spreading her wings
she's a cool, but walking, fire

Her fingertips gliding atop the waves while the breeze
scatters seductive mist

Captivating me with aromas of rose essence, jasmine and
lavender

Charming my ears with ancient lovers' melodies

Stalking toward the shore

Gracefully crushing the soft sand

Arch seductress hypnotizing me with her curvy
pendulum hips

Thrusting her pelvis as fleets of oars on battleships
Spinning on the balls of her feet

Because she knows the center of the universe
is where her thighs meet.

Offering myself to the Black Goddess
and she craves to test my erotic mettle

Her almond shaped eyes requesting I accompany her to
the alter in the temple of fire and desire

Her hand spreads across my chest

Honeysuckled words, long kisses and touches sending
my loins and soul ablaze

We exchange and merge our life-forces
and make love for the remainder of our days.

MIDNIGHT RADIANCE

Haiku

Midnight radiance

Crescent moons watch the lotus

Lay next to lovers

WEE HOURS

He lay restless between his mother and I rolling over
endlessly,
energized in the wee hours of the morning,
propping himself up on her hip,
when the moonlight cast itself through the window
creating a multitude of curiosity for him to investigate.

His cheeks inflating and deflating, blowing rhythmic
melodies of his pacifier

Lifting him up, she places him on his side
so he can only concentrate on her eyes.

He knows her face better than his own,
His uncoordinated hand slides gently over her philtrum
and lips,
rediscovering every seam and grove,

Remeasuring her smile, brightness of her eyes
playing with her hair as if it was his first time.

We know he'll forget this night and many others,
but his first thoughts were incomplete,
knowing only hunger, growth, and solace of mother's
womb.

The vibration he sensed was her voice and heartbeat,

His sight was her feelings.

Mother and Son sharing souls until he departed.

Their bond is unlike anything in the universe.

GIRL ON THE SIDE

I told her to be careful,
showering me with affection in front of my queen.

She knows her kisses are the sweet taste of a quiet
waterfall.

She thinks she's second to none, with uncompromised
loyalty in her eyes watching me.

I'm her sunrises and sunsets.

At night, in secret, I go to her place
holding her tight all night,
we have a unique love affair.

She's passionate, constantly hugging me, rubbing my
face, shoulders, and neck.

She has an immature jealously against the queen
and I make my throne available to her endlessly.

Her voice will always be the heartstring and melody of
my soul.

She's my princess through and through, a perfect
daddy's girl.

PROUD SON OF THE DARK CONTINENT

I wouldn't have survived months of obscurity in the
belly of slave ships
where my kinsmen, sisters and brothers from different
tribes were bombarded with the stench of uncertainty,
tormented by screams of terror from above and within
the dungeon void.

Chained together inside a lair of excrement, surrounded
in the endless pounding of waves against the prison
walls.

Forced to swallow this evil driving,
a few to plunge into the ocean embracing death rather
than servitude.

Many died in vicious rebellions, but the remnants'
suffering was unconceivable.

The atrocities committed by Hades' ferrymen
tenderizing their carcasses
before landing in America.

Led from middle passage prisons to auction blocks
my ancestors' senses were fractured
almost sending them to the brink of madness.

It was only a mental, physical, and spiritual connection that allowed them to endure.

There aren't enough books in history that can be written to express the agony, describe the egregiousness, and transcribe the litany of crimes perpetrated against the people of the Dark Continent.

I wasn't born into bondage,
but shackles were placed on my mind.

I never saw or felt the edge of the overseer's whip, but the world beats and emasculates my image, distorts the legacy of my people and their global contributions.

They label my brothers and I as vagabonds, savage villains and thugs unworthy of recognition or protection.

They rationalize assassinating my character,
revealing a perverted infatuation with me.

It overwhelms them while they are inhaling envy and exhaling my destruction.

Suppressing and oppressing us to a level that our only option is to be moral while living impoverished, starve to death or be a criminal and thrive.

I refuse to submit to being marginalized, provoked,
insulted in order to justify their murderous thirst.

They perceive me as a threat whether I brandish the
sword of manhood or quiet resistance.

They reek with a godly dread of my existence.

TIMIDNESS

I remember the timidness and lack of confidence in your eyes

While people's opinions made you feel like prey and you were insecure with your position.

Sometimes afraid to speak your mind

We reassured you from behind the scenes and backstage when the curtain was down.

Life can be treacherous and joyous,
God ordained the hardships and disappointments.

Our decisions summon unnecessary pain and struggles,
but they all are components of success and failure.

Today
you're a lioness
unrelenting, unapologetic

An assassin pursuing your dreams and aspirations with divine retribution.

Cannibalized your past so that every component is assimilated into a mold

Forging yourself into the tip of the spear
Thrusting yourself through the mist into the field of
battle and conquering it.

SAVANNAH'S AWARD

When her name echoed throughout the auditorium, she thanked and kissed him. Striding with grace toward center stage, her one-of-a-kind, couture pearl-engineered fit, flared French lace illusion. Long sleeves adorned with lace appliques, two elegant magnolia branches resting flawlessly on a slightly plunging sweetheart neckline.

He focused on her eyes and the diamond earrings he gave to her as a sweet sixteen present. After years of persistence and sacrifice, she was being recognized for her career achievements. He reminisced on her journey from childhood into womanhood. It seemed like but a few moments in time. He felt fortunate to have an angel sit on his lap, calling it her throne.

I was barely initiated into manhood when I became your father. But that didn't stop your curiosity. You were my pupil, not my disciple. I gave you love, affection, words of encouragement, and invested money and time. I urged you to do your homework, study, rehearse lines for plays, and routines for cheerleading and pageants. I knew when to apply pressure and when to release it. If I didn't have experience or expertise to guide you, I prayed and God sent a qualified person.

But I saw the divine excellence in you before it was manifested for you and the world to see. I saw your talents in the rawest form, over the years watching you develop your gifts into the extraordinary. I knew it always resonated inside your soul. An overwhelming abundance of energy for life. Your gift for loving others, making your family, friends, peers, children, and elders feel blessed from a small conversation—dynamic nuances that make you distinctive. I caught a glimpse of you while you performed on your first stage at home. Your steps have been ordered by God, but remember everybody won't like the shoes you're wearing in your walk.

I wanted you to discover your own path, because in life, from a distance, the easy, clear path seems to lead to plush valleys and an abundance of resources. However, when you arrive it's overpopulated and carries the stench of mediocrity. The other road is rarely traveled, serrated, covered with mist. Although people who choose this route find limited company, it's the most rewarding to manifest the desires of your soul.

EMPOWER

Empower someone to ignite their passion,
But not at the cost of extinguishing your own.